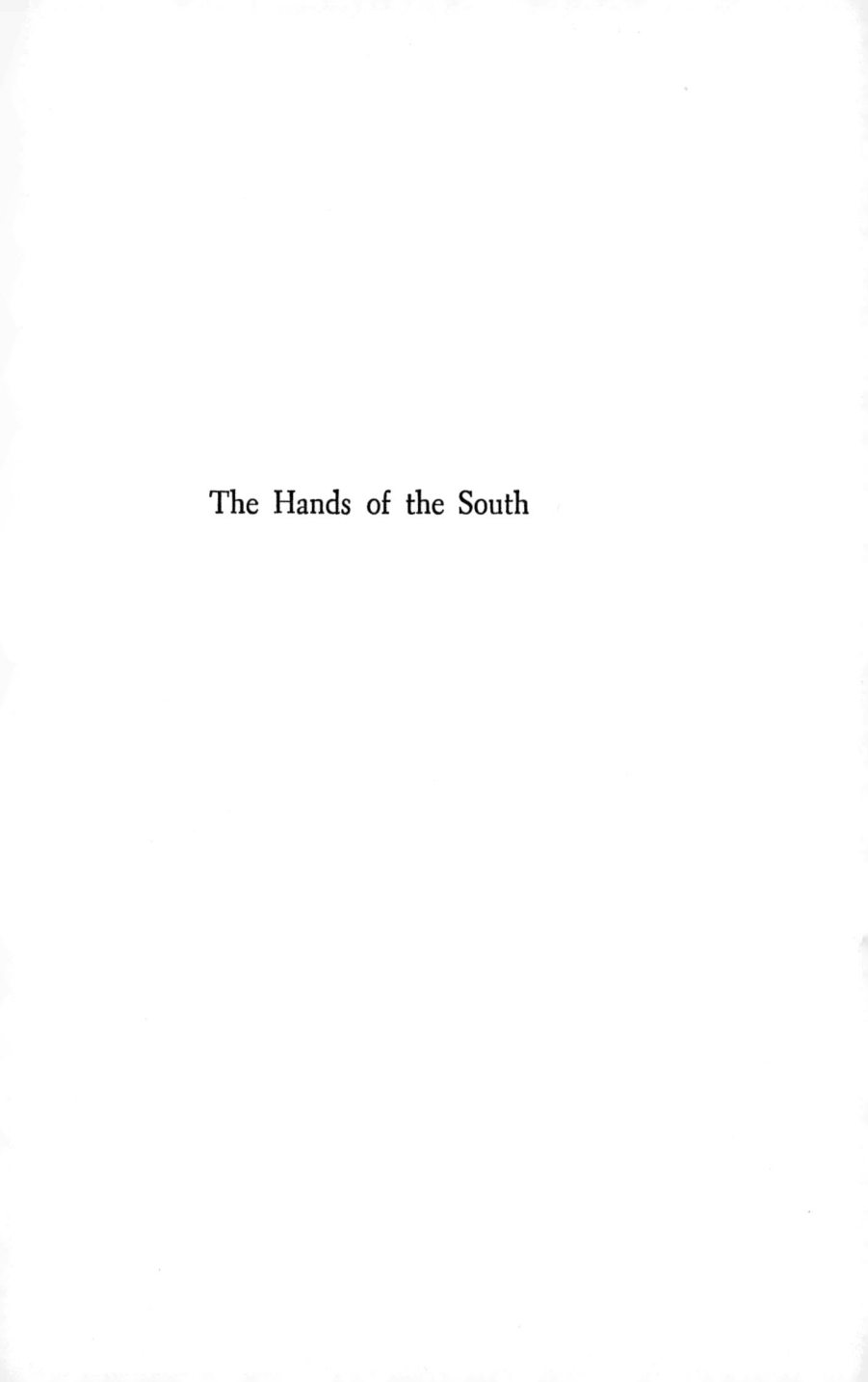

The Hands of the South

THE HANDS OF THE SOUTH

Poems by VITTORIO BODINI

Translations by
Ruth Feldman and Brian Swann

Washington

The Charioteer Press

THIS IS A *Charioteer Book*.

Copyright © 1980 by Ruth Feldman.
Library of Congress Catalog No. 80-68879.
All rights reserved.

No part of this book may be reproduced without permission in writing from the publisher, except by a reviewer who may wish to quote a full poem or passages.

Published by The Charioteer Press.

Manufactured in the United States of America.

FIRST EDITION LIMITED TO 500 COPIES.

ACKNOWLEDGMENTS

Grateful acknowledgment is made to Vittorio Bodini's publisher, Arnoldo Mondadori (Milano); and to *American Poetry Review, Modern Poetry in Translation, New England Review, Poetry Now,* and *Translation,* which published some of these translations.

Publication of this book was supported in part by a grant from the National Endowment for the Arts.

CONTENTS

I

Ma nell'Ora in Cui Tutti Gli Orologi   2
But in the Hour   3
The Trees Were Nourished by the Eyes   4
I Had a Stone   5
Olvido   7
Tobacco Leaves   8

II

Morta in Puglia   16
Dead Woman in Apulia   17
How Much Rage To Exist   18
Xanti-Yaca   19
Moon of the Bourbons   21

III

Finibusterrae   28
Finibusterrae   29
In the Salentine Peninsula   30
Study for the Sanfelice Woman in Jail   31
Lecce   33
Brindisi   34
Via de Angelis   35
Simple Song of Being Oneself   37
The Hands of the South   38

IV

Serie Stazzemese   40
Stazzema Series   41

Poet and Translators   47

The Hands of the South

I

MA NELL'ORA
IN CUI TUTTI GLI OROLOGI

Ma nell'ora in cui tutti gli orologi
si lasciano morire dietro i vetri
come mosche nei freddi dell'autunno,
in quell'ora chi va per i sentieri
di certe folli montagne
d'un piccone ode colpi rintronare
sotto la roccia, uccelli sotterrati
che le grandi ali sbattono, le penne
nere d'echi perdendo, e a quei segnali
un altro che risponde:
ai tuoi segnali, e a tentoni il suo
vuoto innanzi spinge
per farsi incontro, o amata, alle tue vene,
come delitto o musica sepolta.

BUT IN THE HOUR

But in the hour when all the clocks
go dead behind glass
like flies in autumn's cold,
in that hour when the man who walks the paths
of certain mad mountains
hears blows of a pickaxe resound
under the rock, buried birds
that beat great wings, losing
the black feathers of echoes,
and another signal that replies:
at your signals, groping, it pushes
its emptiness ahead, love, to meet your veins,
like a crime or buried music.

THE TREES WERE NOURISHED BY THE EYES

The trees were nourished by the eyes
of mournful birds. All light
had disappeared from the sky
when among the treetrunks I saw fleeing ghosts
burst forth, their breasts pierced
by visible arrows, which they tried
to tear out as they ran.
When dawn gave the trees back their branches
and the leaves their outlines,
a man appeared on a distant path,
around his neck a kerchief
the color of fire. He vanished when I called out.
Then flocks and shepherds passed unaware,
and other people who change seasons
the way you change a sparrow's water.

I HAD A STONE

I had a stone
and this stone had a horizon
and the horizon a wish
to crack, to split
into pomegranates,
into whitewashed walls
according to a plan that was
the plan of my death.

It's with your own death
you must live,
you must accept your own death
like the empty shadow
of a white dog, cut out
of tissue paper
that departs and returns
from its travels in nothingness
and those races, that muzzle
lifted to us,
evoke a certain tenderness.

But now
minus shadow
minus stone how
how shall I know
where I am, to what degree I'm dead
or alive
what things to leave
and what to take.
It's the cave, it's the cave.

It's the cave of the man
with the well-pressed pants.
But do the heavenly skinned knees
of childhood, gloriously wounded,
chase some old
balloon, inflated with
a bicycle pump, intent on
anticipating every false bounce?

And again:
when was it all this began?

OLVIDO

All the clocks in your house
are restless flowers,
or pulse with temples of lemons
in fruit dishes, in the rooms' dark.

What unequal spheres
mark in them is the time
of your split fires: hate and hope,
fear and gratitude, and your years
among which your lovely face passes
moon-quick in the clouds' gaps.

This hand you give me—I don't know
to what day
or what night it belongs;
nor you just how I reached you,
in this rebellious arch over which fly
hours death-stricken by their own deceits.

But if from the dark century of your hair
a carnation falls like a burning star,
everything turns away in flames and memory
confesses its desire to live by that flower.

TOBACCO LEAVES

1

You don't know the South, the whitewashed houses
we came out of into the sun like numbers
from a dice-face.

2

The lunar shell hardly
raises false mountains that look murdered
and a dull shining on the rails,
your name, full of teeth, begins to cry
in the shadow, and bites in the throat
the palm tree and the church of the Rosary.

3

On the plains of the South no dream passes.
Substantives and musicless goats, camped here,
with a sign of the cross on their backs,
or a circle,
wait for another life.
All is evidence and quiet, and one could see
even a thought, a word,
run between two stones
with the gray dismay of a mole.

To gaze at the plain as far as eye can see,
without houses, trees, without a letter:
level of an absence in which
only goats or ghosts of goats dead for centuries stand out,
grazing insomnia's bitter jades,

the lightless steel of ancient swords,
when bitter peoples clashed
and dyed the skies of prehistory with blood.

Thus, if one day from underground
a thin laugh stretches out unleashed
in the sirocco's wind,
what the hoe bares
to unperturbed sky and crows
is the teeth of slain
horses who recall
what a sweet holiday blood made
when it was alive on the plain.

4

When I went back to my Southern village
where everything, every instant of the past
resembles those terrible dead men's wrists
that spring each time from the clods
and, unappeased, eternally tire the spades,
I understood then why I had to lose you:
my face was made here, far from you,
and yours—in other countries I can't picture.

When I went back to my Southern village
I felt myself die.

5

At this hour on Southern earth a sunset
like a butchered animal breaks up.
The air is full of blood,

and the olives, the tobacco leaves.
As yet no light is lit.

A dense whispering, of a thousand voices,
is heard far from the neighboring courtyards:
the whole village wants to show
that it is still alive
in the shadow where a mule-driver reenters
decapitated from the quarries.
How long the dark lasts in the South!
Lights go on late, in houses and streets.
At every cry children
in kitchen gardens add a leaf
to the moon and the basil.

6

Can dusty storks
thread the belltowers' eyes?
Can the exact smile of abstractions
flash from lookouts, through rooms
from which the smell of oranges and lemons and the sirocco's
    wind
bar every memory?
Grown between dry dust and stolen flowers
—jasmine, carnations, and glittering dust—
striplings now tremble in dark passageways
where lascivious fear lures them with its hot breath.
(Every tree was a boundary the train passed
stripping the branches of their foliage of crows;
those black wings, a delirium in the air,
were burnt fragments of a letter
we would try in vain to recompose.)

7

Salentine Bestiary

The light is another beast on the houses
to add to the bestiary
whose fable
smells of spittle and threats,
the gecko, the tarantula,
the aggressive cicada,
the owl.
And that other, which doesn't sing or burn
like the carter's whip
under the cloud of heat
but says grayly: If only things
had been different.
Unclean insect, so melancholy-filled!

8

From the roofs a deadly hand languidly
visits the extinguished ovens, the stalls where
a lantern or dusty voice wakes.
As from a star near death
you hear a song from the tobacco fields.
On the thresholds old women sit, listening,
—or underbrush the moon strikes again in the air—
half-close eyes of an abstract hardness,
the palms of their hands stones, open on laps.

9

Cuatros Caminos

What nervous silence
what a miserable dream
of coal and mud in the suburbs!
Between bedraggled houses an occasional gas lamp
throws its greenish shadow onto the shadow:
there a couple disappears, and where they vanished,
a snake's tail flashes for an instant
among the reeds of a remote summer.

A senseless pity
dry as sunflower seeds
whirls in crowds at the crossroads,
while in your land invisible
peasants speak dark blue
from the tobacco fields, and in an instant
the night will taste of green olive.

10

Blows rain on sleeping houses.
The moon springs from them,
and the blue born in corollas, in passageways.

We speak of the logos and of love,
passing our houses more than once,
the notebooks of beds where every sum has already been reckoned,
and the golden fish that will escape from our breasts in sleep,
swimming through the room's dark
and pronouncing the obscure sentences of dreams.

But you, moon, light
the unknown windows of the North,
while we talk here,
in the depths of this exiled province
where only the nape of your neck is visible.

11

We live enchanted
among tufa palaces
in a great plain.
On the shores of nothingness
we show the caverns of ourselves
—some palm trees, a saint
bloodstained by the sunsets, a slow
book of few facts, which we read
again and again, waiting for it to give
all together the life
the things we think are due us.

12

A pugnacious monk flies between the trees.*

---

* The conformist biographers of the saints draw an edifying picture of the youth of San Giuseppe da Copertino, but the portrait Fremautius gives us is much more plausible for a youth of Copertino: *audacis iracundaeque indolis*, spoiling for a fight and ready to hurl himself upon the first comer with his fists, and where they were not enough, with a knife. This seventeenth century saint of Lecce was not overburdened with brains, but all he needed was to hear an organ play, or to look at an image of the Madonna, in order immediately (while murmuring "Mater mea", *emisso suspiro*) to rise from the ground, reaching a height of nearly a hundred yards at times. Of those more substantial flights and ecstasies, leaving aside the minor ones that took place normally during prayers, more than seventy, *plus quam septuaginta*, were testified to by witnesses.

II

MORTA IN PUGLIA

Quando seppe l'aumento del prezzo dei pomodori
capì che il tempo dei palpiti era finito.
Imparò a brontolare
e a mettere le mani nella lisciva bollente.
Nella casa imbiancata da poco tempo
ardeva su una parete
un serto di pepe diavolo per i maschi.
All'alba un muratore uscì tossendo
e chiuse l'uscio di casa,
le foglie di limone dentro il cuscino
ricordarono un sole di giallo d'ossa.

Morta, non morire di più.
Ricordati delle ulive nere.
Lucida le maniglie e annaffia i garofani.

Dimentica che i vetri delle finestre
si lavano con acqua e aceto;
che le macchie sui vestiti scuri
si tolgono con la posa del caffè.
Non è più tua la mano che destina ad altro uso
la cera ancora molle dei candelieri
o che scalda sul gas la cioccolata dei morti.
Risorgi nell'Inutile, morta in Puglia:
nei coralli del mare o negli urli del vento
nella tua terra d'ostriche e di lupi mannari.

DEAD WOMAN IN APULIA

When she learned how tomatoes had gone up in price
she knew the time for love was past.
She learned to grumble
and plunge her hands in boiling lye.
In the newly whitewashed house
a garland of red-hot peppers
burned on the wall for the men.
At dawn a mason went out coughing
and closed the front door;
the lemon leaves in the pillow
recalled a bone-yellow sun.

Dead woman, don't die any more.
Remember the black olives.
Polish the doorknobs and water the carnations.

Forget that windows
are washed with water and vinegar;
that spots on dark clothing
are removed with coffee grounds.
No longer is it your hand that turns
the still-soft wax of candlesticks to another use
or heats the chocolate of the dead over the gas flame.
Rise from the dead in the Useless, dead woman in Apulia:
in the sea corals, or the howling of the wind,
in your land of oysters and werewolves.

HOW MUCH RAGE TO EXIST

How much rage to exist turns into love!
Here you would have to cite cases, tell
and retell, choose in the mirrors
of leaves, water, snow. Once I wanted to know
how an otter's head with a fleshless fishbone
can laugh in the moon
—what would the moon have thought of that sight—
and this desire was love. Elves with
comical big caps of hair
twisted the horses' tails into plaits.
In a small street named after an obscure battle,
she thought I was going to kill her.
Now, far away, she laughs at all that
while, drunk, she stares into the bottom of a glass or the sea.
But distance can prolong itself at will,
can make a vague hypothesis of remorse.
Surely you too have stopped here sometimes at night
under a balcony or a tree,
listening to the Italian cricket sing,
and, at that sudden interruption of your steps,
open false furrows, pushing the song away from itself
as though it were distant, or fall silent
then suddenly start up again from another illusory point.

6

The village priests
have dirty shoes,
green teeth, and live
with nieces.
Next to empty
collection boxes
Christ bleeds Bourbon red
from his wounds;
a harsh agony
rises from benches
and wildflowers.
In the piazza, huddled
on the knees of the Town Hall,
the unemployed
take the sun's gold.

In the black South
a skinny tomcat trots confidently.

7

Strokes slowly
detach themselves
from a clock and swim
among rain, wind and windowpanes.
Terraces drum
like tent canvas
and the shout of children—"Aea!"—is lost
in the streets
as through the corridors
of a castle under siege.

Besieging winter,
the year's old age,
fills the senses with anguish,
shuts out tomorrow.

But let's leave this city for a moment.
Let's slide into sleep,
let's go and see what's happening.

8

I wouldn't want to die here
where I have to live, my town
so undesirable I can't help loving you;
slow plain where light looks
like raw meat
and the medlar tree comes and goes between us and winter.

Lazy
as a half-moon in the May sun,
the cup of coffee, the wasted words,
I live now in the things my eyes can see:
I become olive tree and wheel of a slow cart,
hedge of prickly pear, bitter soil
where the tobacco grows.
But you, deadly and troubled, so much mine,
so alone,
you say it isn't true; that isn't all there is.
Sad envy of living;
in this whole plain
there's not one branch on which you'd want to perch.

9

Cocumola

A village called Cocumola
is
like having your hands dirtied by flour,
and a small lemon-green door.
Men in silent shirts
tie knots in their neckerchiefs
to remember their hearts.
The tobacco is drying,
and life cocumolates among the pots and pans
where feathered women are tasting the broth.

10

Sea, when you resume dominion
over this sullen province,
your thin knife blades
will strip millenial seashells,
your lost signets, from our tufa,
and the dolphin with the half-moon in its mouth*
will call us by name,
as now, between four tapers, hired mourners
lament lives without horses, without love.
The coast might be down there, where crickets sing,
where crickets say "Jesu! Jesu!"

---

* The dolphin with the half-moon in its mouth is the coat-of-arms of the Terra d'Otranto, formerly the territory of Norman counts.

11

And in the end orange trees, heavy, festooned with flags;
thorns and gusts
of sweetness among the prickly pears; men
swaying on empty carts,
going to load tufa
from the quarries,
their dogs dead with sleep.
And seasons with the tapered beaks
of storks, that pick fleas from their breasts,
lift stones from the ground
and throw them farther away.

III

FINIBUSTERRAE

Vorrei essere fieno sul finire del giorno
portato alla deriva
fra campi di tabacco e ulivi, su un carro
che arriva in un paese dopo il tramonto
in un'aria di gomma scura.
Angeli pterodattili sorvolano
quello stretto cunicolo in cui il giorno
vacilla: è un'ora
che è peggio solo morire, e sola luce
è accesa in piazza una sala da barba.
Il fanale d'un camion,
scopa d'apocalisse, va scoprendo
crolli di donne in fuga
nel vano delle porte e tornerà
il bianco per un attimo a brillare
della calce, regina arsa e concreta
di questi umili luoghi dove termini,
meschinamente, Italia, in poca rissa
d'acque ai piedi d'un faro.
E qui che i salentini dopo morti
fanno ritorno
col cappello in testa.

FINIBUSTERRAE

I wish I were hay at day's end,
drifting
among tobacco and olive fields, on a cart
that arrives in a village after sunset
in dark rubbery air.
Pterodactyllic angels hover above
that narrow tunnel where day
flickers: it's the worst hour
in which to die alone. In the piazza
the only light is in the barbershop.
The headlight of a truck,
apocalyptic furze, reveals
women collapsing in flight
in doorways, and whiteness
will return for an instant to shine
with the whitewash, burnt concrete queen
of these humble places where, Italy,
you end meanly in a small riot
of waters at the foot of a lighthouse.
This is the place to which Salentines return
after death,
hats on heads.

IN THE SALENTINE PENINSULA

Love was a letter found
in the trunk of an olive tree; friendship
the hair split in two, blown
away by the wind; and death
was the tooth you save for the Day
of Judgment.

Here there were academies
and most learned monks:
O glorious cities
of filth and abandon!
In the mornings manless women
suckle their babies on doorsteps
or comb their hair endlessly.
And what black hair, what
never-ending hair,
among those white houses with the rows
of yellow squash on the cornices!

On a garbage heap a fierce cat
nibbled at a mother-of-pearl fishbone,
watching the approaching stranger
with its two terrible eyes.

STUDY FOR THE SANFELICE
WOMAN IN JAIL

At the time of the Bourbons
women were little skeins of silk;
let us not speak of hearts of chicory,
or the dense jewels of doves
that came and went
like slaps in the air around the churches.

But at the iron gratings that give onto
damp courtyards
the boys sniffed green and silence.
What a point of departure for their dreams!
They scratched at the green with their eyes,
at silence with their hands.

At times gold lemons were stars
in those skies imprisoned by
a worm-eaten door, beyond which
the needle seller passed with his shout,
the seller of squash seeds cried his wares,
the milk vendor's trumpet was heard,
and that of the kerosene vendor
with the trained donkey.
This was the climate of the times: Human lives
scanned the beat of other lives,
but for the boys with their eyes
lost in the imprisoned green, that seldom
rustled, each of those cries, each sound,
unique, beyond reason,
was detached from the day's texture.

Not for her, no: not for the Sanfelice woman
in jail;
out of everything—every voice
every thought—she made a quiet
watchful thread for her soft embroidery.
Will that human dreaming of hers
find safekeeping in the silence?
She will find it in the white and blue plaster,
and the door's wood will be that much more wood:
everything will be more itself
if she continues her quiet embroidering.

LECCE

A white gilt
sky where angels
with soft breasts
run along cornices;
Saracen soldiers and learned donkeys
with elaborate ruffs.

A frenetic play
of the spirit that fears
time,
multiplies figures,
defends itself
against a too-bright day.

A soft unhurried
golden air
lingers in that kingdom
of unserviceable cogs among which
boredom's seed
opens its gruffly witty flowers
and as though on a bet
a carnival of stone
simulates infinity in a thousand guises.

BRINDISI

The last sun on the carts
and on the horses' tails,
the last sun of today
which is not tomorrow.

The mule-drivers
at the fountain with their pails
turned their backs
on that oval almost exiled mirror
in which evening lowered its nets
and a violet of oblivion, and nesting
in some parts of the waves
small seagulls
asked for the story
of Moby Dick, who moves alone
over absolute oceans.

There was a palm tree guarding the fountain
I was watching like a thief.
Thief of time that robs us so.
It was here the Crusaders
watered their horses.

VIA DE ANGELIS

Paraffin, goddess of the little table —
I thought your heart
was made of soft wax—
and a pail of dark water
where shoe uppers are soaking,
the tomatoes' red,
the black of the coal cellar,
all salute me. Street
without equal, how you sing in my heart,
and how they've grown,
the little daughters of whores
whose mothers I once saw delousing them
with rare raucousness
in their free moments!
In circumspect skirts
the flesh grows languid: will they too know
the wine and the geranium,
the furtive calls, sudden
clamor at night? And later, in the morning,
the nuns: shining and dense
voices flew, arrows clusters of gold
from the convent of the Carmelites.
If they went out into the street,
it was useless to look
into their eyes
into those lovely faces
of women meant to be peasants ...
useless to try to guess
who had flushed like wild game that song
all made of gold or strawberry or mint.

This crooked road, my skin
was reeling then,
stones and human paving
whose smell and gray sadness
got into my blood.
Having left the world, outside the game,
as I believed myself to be,
away from its closed competitions
of trains and egotism,
of enduring or imposing,
I was like a cat that appears
in the light from the cellars' darkness
with a terrible look
as if it had come back from discovering
a passage through hell.
The whitewash and the sonorous sky,
the poor reality of your strange recompense
were more than I deserved:
an irony
that consoled me, so I smiled
at every lost thing.
You guided my glance through every door,
through everyone else's life:
I have lived
at every street number
with everyone
with the swallows,
the old people who die at dawn
in a green watery light,
with the evicted
riding with their belongings on a cart,
the windowpanes
and the lemon tree in the courtyard.

SIMPLE SONG OF BEING ONESELF

The ivy tells me: you'll never
be ivy. And the wind:
you won't be wind. And the sea:
you won't be sea.

Rags, rivers, bridal dawn
tell me: you won't be rag or river,
you won't be bridal dawn.

The anchor, the four of diamonds, the sofa bed
tell me: you won't be us,
you never have been.

And so say dream, arch, peninsula,
spiderweb, espresso machine.

The mirror says:
how can you be a mirror
if all you give back is your own image?

Things say: try to be yourself
without us.
Spare us your love.

Delicately I flee from everything.
I try to stay alone. I find
death, fear.

THE HANDS OF THE SOUTH

for Rafael Alberti

You have done well he says not to speak to me of the South
of the South and its naked goats leaping from rock to rock

O the pale hands of the goats of the South

You have done well he says not to speak to me of the South
of the South and its goats half devoured by the State

O the white nails of the goats of the South

You have done well he says not to speak to me of the South
of the South and its horizons once open in every direction

O the bloodless nails with which everyone lacerates himself in the South

You have done well he says not to speak to me of the South
of the South and its day-laborers killed by the police

O the pale plump hands of the Tribunals of the South
the olives with human hearts the merciless accusing and
accusing of The Great South on questions of principle

You have done well not to speak to me of the South

IV

SERIE STAZZEMESE

1

Ninetta porta il vecchio
cavallo che fu da corsa
ai monti Apuani. Fissa
il posto, la pensione, torna
con la siecento, triste (a Cècina
un polletto le è andato fra le ruote).

2

Ninetta, la poesia
(d'estate) è un pappagallo
dalle penne oro e verdi e una mania
di contraddire.
Così mentre tu sogni
d'arrivare in Versilia
in regola, coi pantaloni gialli,
io penso a un viaggio di sei anni fa.
Ballava la Olivetti,
la bombola del gas
sopra il sedile posteriore, il trucco
troppo forte ti sbilanciava il viso —
poi l'arrivo a un paese
dove moriva il giorno
come un gran gallo suicida
sulle terrazze.

STAZZEMA SERIES

1

Ninetta brings the old
horse that was running
in the Apuan mountains. She settles on
a place, lodgings, returns
in a Fiat 600, sad (at Cècina
a small chicken got under the wheels).

2

Ninetta, poetry
(in summer) is a parrot
with gold and green feathers and a mania
for contradiction.
So while you dream
of arriving at Versilia
conventionally, in yellow pants,
I think of a trip I took six years ago.
The Olivetti was dancing,
with the bottled gas
on the back seat, too much
makeup threw your face off balance—
then the arrival at a town
where day was
like a big rooster committing suicide
on the terraces.

3

TARQUINIA

(A memory of Cardarelli*)

Here the false Etruscan, the man
with the lifted forefinger
and no other faith but that
in the marble of the word,
studied the yellow of the roof tiles
subdued by the sky.
The pale aluminum walls
were behind his words
while he was dying, soiled
and furious swan,
among the tables on Via Veneto,
and slightly less the sleek fountains
like women's bellies,
and the little doors
with metal curtains to keep mosquitoes out.
These were more or less
the lights of Tarquinia that he kept in his heart,
the false Etruscan and true
despiser of the world
when, finger raised, he spoke to you
at Tito Magri's
or drank Frascati wine.

---

* An Italian poet who was born in Tarquinia in 1887, and in 1906 moved to Rome, where he worked at menial jobs at first, later publishing poetry and prose and acting as contributor to, and finally editor of, various literary magazines.

4

I matured late. It's the mania
for living too fast that betrayed me.
Not giving time to time. Seeing
beauty and suffering
at not being able to use it.
I learned late to tune the heart's motions
to the murmuring of a brook,
to admit nature to my thoughts
like a guest left to his own devices.

5

There is Mount Forato
with the ring in its nose.
Tissue-paper hearts
trembled in the woods
for San Rocco.
The band piled out of the truck
and played in the pagoda,
while the old men of Stazzema
beat time to the *coda*.

6

GREEN BOREDOM KILLS

The mosses, the maidenhair fern,
the blackberries' small red heads,
the hen that silently
moves her trembling mouth
like an empty figure

moving farther and farther away in a dream,
they have dispelled
all private concerns. To ask oneself:
"At what point am I my own man?"
is senseless.
Green boredom kills
idolatrous hearts.
The sandal slips
from the foot,
the jacket snags
on a bramble.
Here I am turned into
a wood. I will be
only one thread among so many
of this green tapestry behind which
an invisible shepherdess
pleads with an invisible she-goat.

7

MONSTERS

Death and discontent have returned.
The goats run round the mountain
at breakneck speed,
and a plumed serpent,
made of rubber, is crouched
in the middle of the road.

8

THIS GREEN TELEGRAPH

This green telegraph among the grasses—
what will it say? And the dry
chestnut-tree leaf that seems to fall
on the heart's ancient wounds?
You see the angry outlines
of the rocks fallen impetuously
from the peaks into the valley's depths
where the torrent makes harps of them,
decorating them with moss, and the air
freshens itself in those leaps
between the burning red and black of the blackberries
and the little skirts of ivy round the trunks.

POET AND TRANSLATORS

VITTORIO BODINI was born in Bari in 1914 and died in Rome in 1970. He lived and worked in Madrid from 1946 to 1950, later becoming professor of Spanish languages and literature at the University of Bari and the University of Pescara. Bodini published five books of poems, winning the Carducci and the Tarquinia Cardarelli Prizes. He translated Cervantes, Quevedo, Lorca, Salinas, and Alberti.

In his poetry Bodini took for subject matter the world of the Italian South, of his native Apulia, its vivid landscapes and its people. Its whole history—Greek, Roman, Byzantine, Norman, Swabian, Spanish — was Bodini's own history. His poems, which combine elements of surrealism and a touch of the baroque, are, as his translators Ruth Feldman and Brian Swann say, "full of dark corners and strange shapes seen as though for the first time."

RUTH FELDMAN and BRIAN SWANN are well known for their collaborative poetry translations. Volumes of their translations of poems of Piccolo, Zanzotto, and Scotellaro have been published by Princeton University Press, of Cattafi by Ardis, of Levi by Menard. The latter book won the John Florio Prize for the best Italian translations published in the United Kingdom in 1976. The translators' anthology *Italian Poetry Today* (New Rivers) was published in 1979.

Feldman, who is both poet and painter, lives in Cambridge, Massachusetts, with long annual sojourns in Italy. Her poems and her poetry translations done independently have appeared in leading magazines in the United States; translations of many of her poems have been published in Italy. Her book *The Ambition of Ghosts* (1979) was published by Green River Press.

Swann's poetry and fiction have been published widely. His third book of poems, *Living Time* (Quarterly Review of Literature), came out in 1979. Another book of poems, three books of fiction, and Euripides' *The Phoenician Women* translated with Peter Burian are scheduled for 1980. Swann is Associate Professor at The Cooper Union.

This book was composed on the Linotype
in Electra and printed by
Theo. Gaus, Ltd., Brooklyn, N.Y. 11201.